Here Is the Coral Reef

Madeleine Dunphy

ILLUSTRATED BY

Tom Leonard

Web of Life

CHILDREN'S BOOKS

*H*ere is the coral reef.

*H*ere is the coral
of all colors and shapes
that lives in clear waters
in this vivid seascape:
Here is the coral reef.

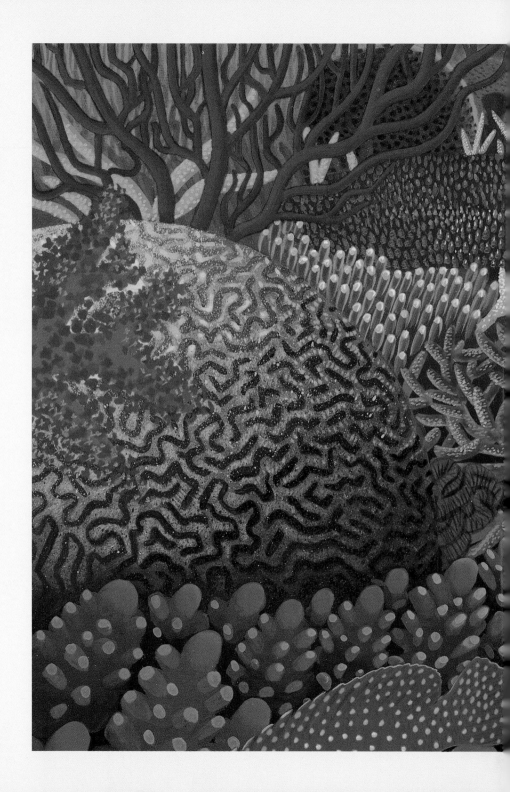

*H*ere are the parrotfish
who eat the coral
of all colors and shapes
that lives in clear waters
in this vivid seascape:
Here is the coral reef.

*H*ere are the wrasses

that clean the parrotfish

who eat the coral

of all colors and shapes

that lives in clear waters

in this vivid seascape:

Here is the coral reef.

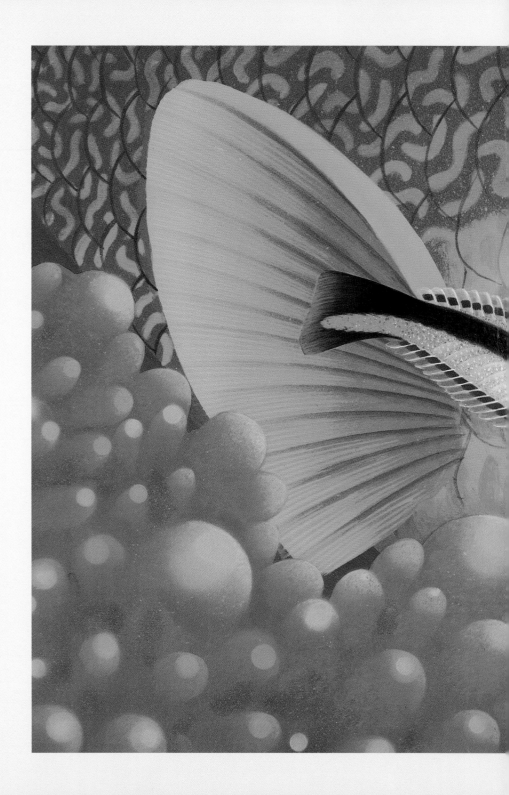

Here is the cod

who is groomed by the wrasses

that clean the parrotfish

who eat the coral

of all colors and shapes

that lives in clear waters

in this vivid seascape:

Here is the coral reef.

Here is the anemone
that stings the cod
who is groomed by the wrasses
that clean the parrotfish
who eat the coral
of all colors and shapes
that lives in clear waters
in this vivid seascape:
Here is the coral reef.

Here are the clownfish

who hide in the anemone

that stings the cod

who is groomed by the wrasses

that clean the parrotfish

who eat the coral

of all colors and shapes

that lives in clear waters

in this vivid seascape:

Here is the coral reef.

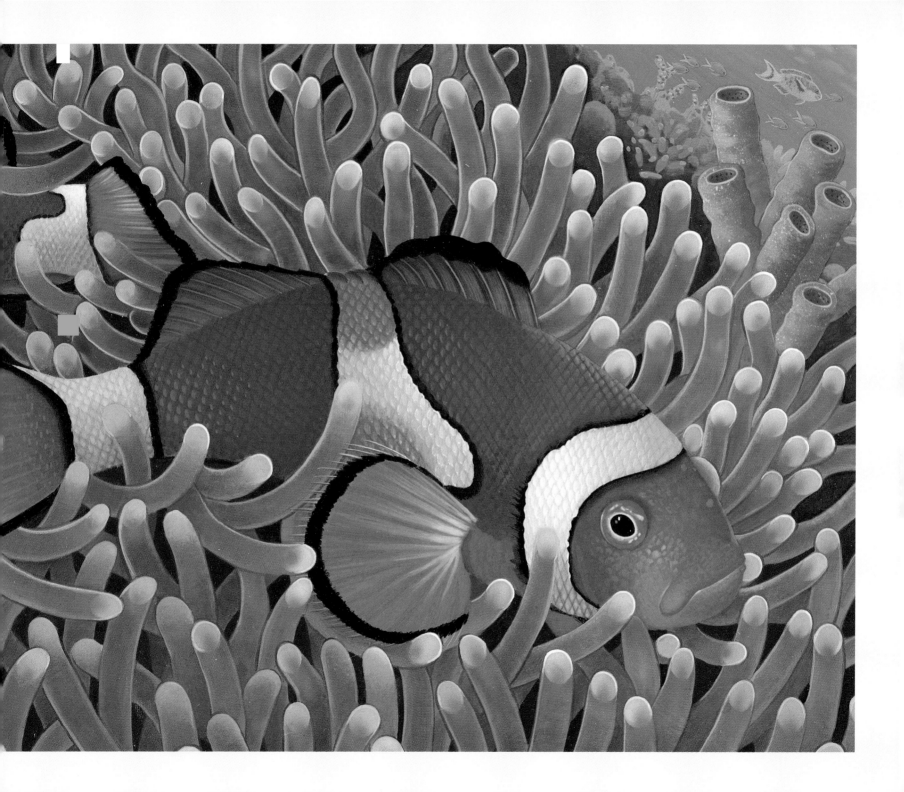

*H*ere is the sponge

that lives near the clownfish

who hide in the anemone

that stings the cod

who is groomed by the wrasses

that clean the parrotfish

who eat the coral

of all colors and shapes

that lives in clear waters

in this vivid seascape:

Here is the coral reef.

Here is the turtle

that nibbles the sponge

that lives near the clownfish

who hide in the anemone

that stings the cod

who is groomed by the wrasses

that clean the parrotfish

who eat the coral

of all colors and shapes

that lives in clear waters

in this vivid seascape:

Here is the coral reef.

*H*ere is the ray

who swims with the turtle

that nibbles the sponge

that lives near the clownfish

who hide in the anemone

that stings the cod

who is groomed by the wrasses

that clean the parrotfish

who eat the coral

of all colors and shapes

that lives in clear waters

in this vivid seascape:

Here is the coral reef.

*H*ere are the remoras

that ride the ray

who swims with the turtle

that nibbles the sponge

that lives near the clownfish

who hide in the anemone

that stings the cod

who is groomed by the wrasses

that clean the parrotfish

who eat the coral

of all colors and shapes

that lives in clear waters

in this vivid seascape:

Here is the coral reef.

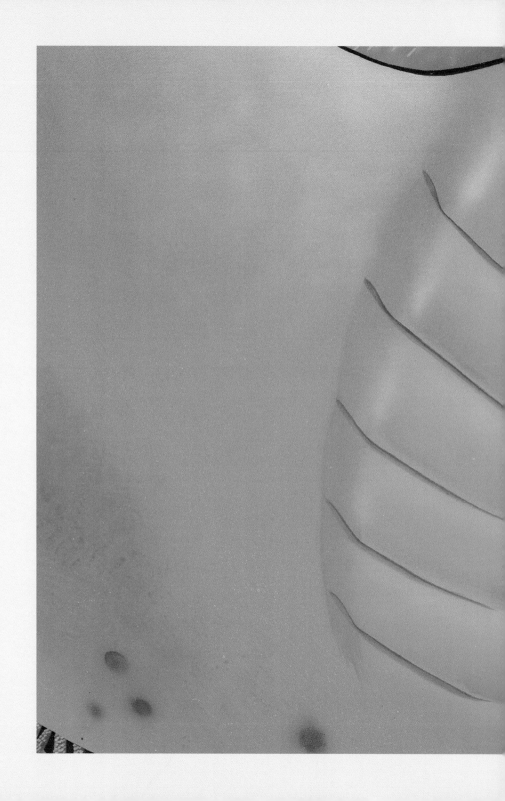

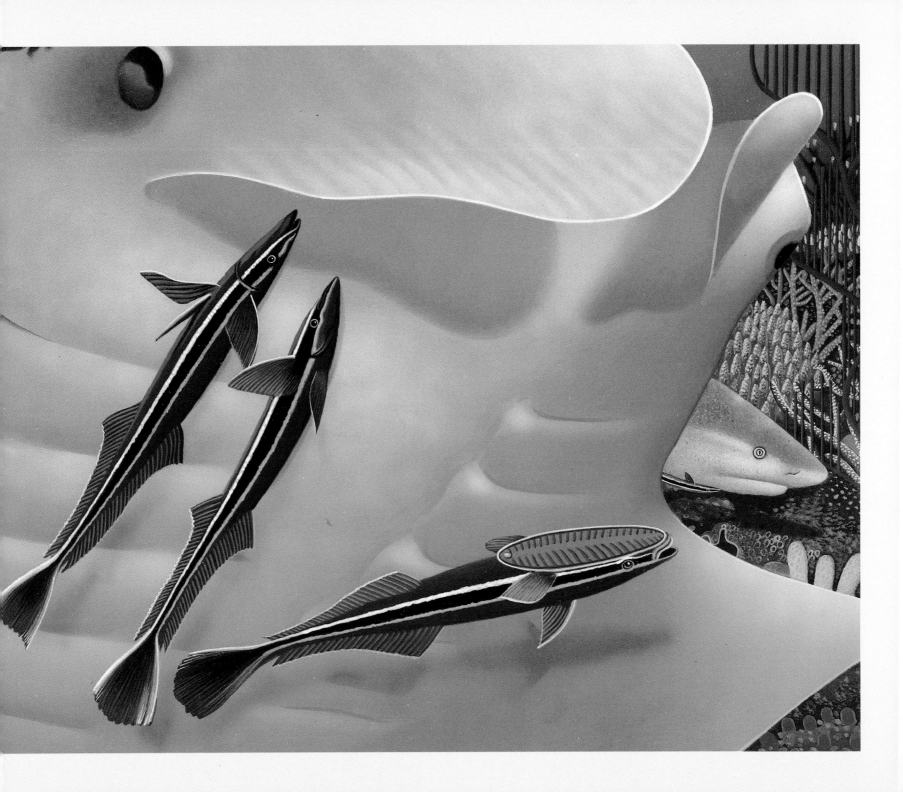

*H*ere is the shark

that carries the remoras

that ride the ray

who swims with the turtle

that nibbles the sponge

that lives near the clownfish

who hide in the anemone

that stings the cod

who is groomed by the wrasses

that clean the parrotfish

who eat the coral

of all colors and shapes

that lives in clear waters

in this vivid seascape:

Here is the coral reef.

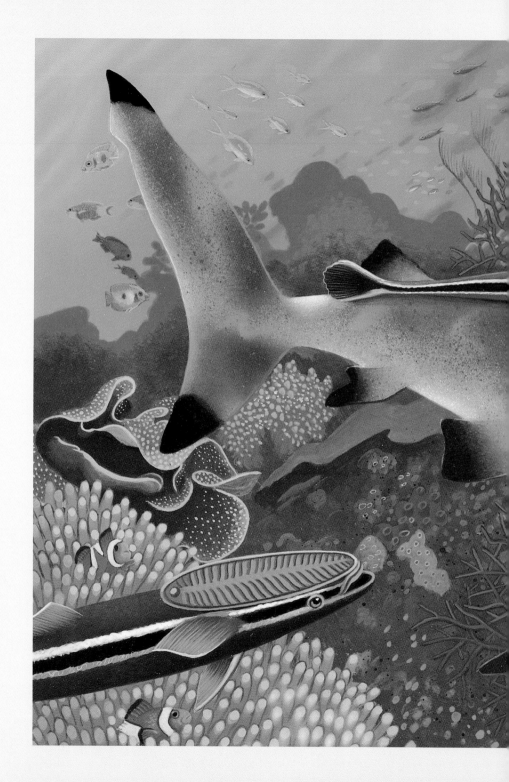

Here is the eel

who is attacked by the shark

that carries the remoras

that ride the ray

who swims with the turtle

that nibbles the sponge

that lives near the clownfish

who hide in the anemone

that stings the cod

who is groomed by the wrasses

that clean the parrotfish

who eat the coral

of all colors and shapes

that lives in clear waters

in this vivid seascape:

Here is the coral reef.

Here is the coral

that shelters the eel

who is attacked by the shark

that carries the remoras

that ride the ray

who swims with the turtle

that nibbles the sponge

that lives near the clownfish

who hide in the anemone

that stings the cod

who is groomed by the wrasses

that clean the parrotfish

who eat the coral

of all colors and shapes

that lives in clear waters

in this vivid seascape:

Here is the coral reef.

Wildlife of the Great Barrier Reef

MORAY EEL

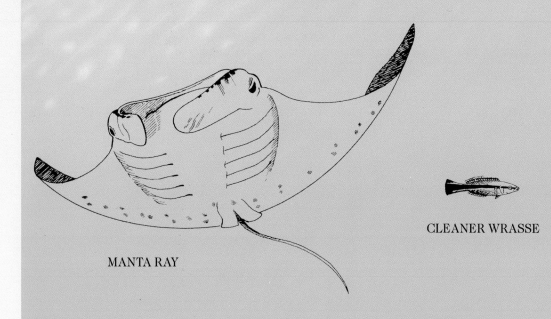

MANTA RAY

CLEANER WRASSE

PARROTFISH

ANEMONE

The creatures shown in this book live in Australia's Great Barrier Reef. Coral reefs also exist in the Caribbean Sea, Red Sea, Indian Ocean, and in other tropical seas where the water is warm, clear, salty, and fairly shallow. Coral reefs have more species of animals and plants than any other underwater environment.

Coral may look like a colorful rock, but it is actually a living animal. Coral is built from the joined skeletons of tiny creatures called polyps. Most coral polyps are smaller than a pea. Many plants and animals depend on coral for food and shelter.

One unusual looking animal that lives in the coral reef is the sea anemone. The only animals that can safely touch the anemone's stinging tentacles are anemone fish, also known as clownfish. When a clownfish first approaches an anemone it makes light contact until the fish becomes desensitized to the anemone's sting.

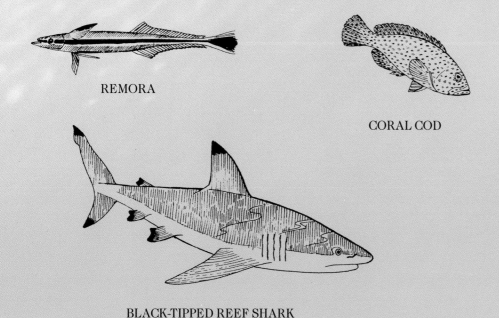

REMORA

CORAL COD

HAWKSBILL TURTLE

BLACK-TIPPED REEF SHARK

CLOWNFISH

If the clownfish feels threatened, it retreats into the anemone's tentacles where it is safe from predators.

The sponge is another animal that lives in the coral reef. Most people think of the sponge as something to use in the bathroom, without realizing that they are scrubbing themselves with an animal's skeleton.

Coral reefs face a number of threats such as pollution, destructive fishing practices, and global warming. We must act now to help ensure the survival of coral reefs. To find out what you can do, write to The Coral Reef Alliance, 417 Montgomery Street, Suite 205, San Francisco, CA 94104, or visit their website at www.coralreefalliance.org.

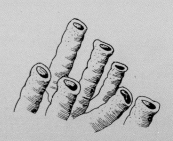

SPONGE

For Chris, with love.
—M.D.

For my parents, Richard and Theresa.
—T.L.

Text ©2007 by Madeleine Dunphy.
Illustrations ©1998 by Tom Leonard.

First published in 1998 by Hyperion Books for Children.

For information, write to:
Web of Life Children's Books
P.O. Box 2726, Berkeley, California 94702

Published in the United States in 2007 by Web of Life Children's Books.

Printed in Singapore.

Library of Congress Control Number: 2006924062

ISBN 0-9773795-4-X (paperback edition)
978-0-9773795-4-5

ISBN 0-9773795-5-8 (hardcover edition)
978-0-9773795-5-2

The artwork for this book was prepared using acrylic.

Read all the books in the series:
Here Is the African Savanna, Here Is the Tropical Rain Forest, Here Is the Wetland,
Here Is the Southwestern Desert, Here Is the Arctic Winter, and *Here Is Antarctica.*

For more information about our books, and the authors
and artists who create them, visit our website:
www.weboflifebooks.com

Distributed by Publishers Group West
(800)788-3123
www.pgw.com